10 NO-GRID SURVIVAL HACKS

YOU SHOULD KNOW

Basic Projects, BIG Change,
Wherever You Live

Dennis Carson

For more information, visit the publisher's website at www.offgridlivinghacks.com.

Published by Off Grid Living Hacks

Printed in the United States of America

First Edition: January 2024

CONTENTS

1

SMALL CANDLES, LASTING WARMTH

USE TERRACOTTA POTS AND CANDLES TO CREATE
A SMALL SPACE HEATER

Candle powered heaters are a charming way to add a little extra warmth to your space. This method may seem a touch old-fashioned, but there's a reason it's still around: it's simple, effective, and has a certain rustic charm. Using just candles and terracotta pots, you can create a small source of heat that's perfect for those days when there's a bit of a chill in the air.

The concept is straightforward, yet it has an almost magical feel to it, turning the simple act of lighting a candle into a way to warm your surroundings. It's a cost-effective and enjoyable project that not only heats but also adds a cozy, inviting glow to any room.

How Does It Work?

How heat is generated from candles

Let's take a quick look into the science behind our candle heater. Lighting a candle starts a small combustion process, where the wax is drawn up the wick, vaporizes, and then burns, releasing heat. Usually, this heat just rises and dissipates, but we're going to capture and utilize it more effectively with our setup.

The role of terracotta pots

Terracotta pots are not just decorative; they're the workhorse of the candle heater. When placed over the candles, these pots absorb the heat, hold onto it, and then gently release it back into the room. The result is a more consistent and distributed heat source, taking the relatively small flame of a candle and turning it into a mini radiator.

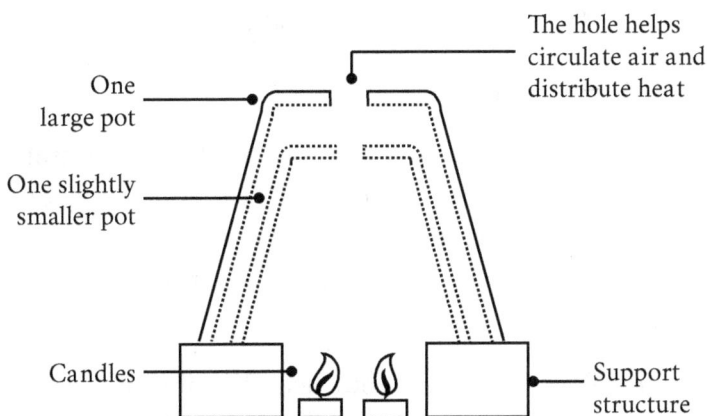

The hole helps circulate air and distribute heat

One large pot

One slightly smaller pot

Candles

Support structure

Safety considerations and efficiency tips

While building and using a candle powered heater is generally safe, a few precautions are necessary. Always keep an eye on it, especially if you're moving around or have pets or kids. Ensure it's on a sturdy, non-flammable surface, and keep flammable items at a safe distance. And don't forget ventilation – it's crucial to maintain good airflow to avoid any buildup of fumes, including carbon monoxide.

To maximize the efficiency of your heater, choose high-quality, long-lasting candles and experiment with the number and placement of candles and pots. Remember, while this won't replace your main heating system, it's a delightful way to add extra warmth and ambiance to your home.

Materials and Tools Needed

Before you dive into creating your cozy, candle-powered heater, let's talk about what you'll need to gather. The beauty of this project is in its simplicity and the fact that you might already have some of these items lying around your home.

List of materials

Candles: The heart of your heater. You'll want to grab some sturdy, long-lasting candles. Tealights are commonly used due to their size and burn time, but any candle will do the trick. Just remember, the more candles you use, the more heat you'll generate.

Terracotta Pots: These are your heat distributors. You'll need one large terracotta pot and one slightly smaller one that can fit inside the larger. The hole at the bottom of the pot is crucial as it helps circulate air and distribute heat.

Base: This is a stable, heat-resistant surface for placing your candles. This could be a metal tray or ceramic plate, situated in a safe location away from any flammable materials.

Support Structure Materials: You'll need materials to create a stable, elevated structure around the candles. This can include bricks or metal hardware that can withstand heat and is taller than the candles. The structure should be stable enough to support the weight of the terracotta pots.

Tools for assembling your heater

Lighter or Matches: To get those candles burning.

Heat Resistant Gloves: When handling the pots after they've been heated, you'll want these to protect your hands.

Optional - Paint: If you want to get fancy, you can paint your terracotta pots to match your decor. Just make sure you're using heat-resistant paint!

Where to find these materials

Candles and Terracotta Pots: These can be found at most home goods stores, garden centers, or craft stores. If you're looking to save a bit or be more sustainable, check out local thrift stores or online marketplaces for second-hand options.

Support Structure Materials: You might find suitable materials around your house, such as bricks, unused kitchen hardware, or metal crafting supplies. Make sure whatever you choose is heat-resistant, non-flammable, and sturdy. Just ensure it's stable and non-flammable.

Once you've gathered all your materials and tools, you're all set to start building your heater. Remember, this is supposed to be a fun and straightforward project, so don't stress too much about getting everything perfect. Use what you have, be creative, and most importantly, stay safe while you assemble and enjoy your new source of warmth.

Step-by-Step Guide to Building Your Heater

Now that you've got all your materials ready, let's roll up our sleeves and build this nifty little heater. Follow these steps to safely assemble and enjoy the warmth of your new candle-powered heater.

Step 1: Setting up candles

Candle Arrangement: Arrange your candles on the base. If you're using tealights, you can arrange them close together for a concentrated heat source. For larger candles, ensure they're stable and upright.

Support Structure: Create a support structure around the candles using bricks, metal stands, or any sturdy, non-flammable material. This structure should be taller than the candles and stable enough to support the terracotta pots.

Light 'Em Up: Once your candles are set and the support structure is in place, light the candles. Make sure each one is burning steadily before moving on to the next step.

Step 2: Assembling the terracotta pots

Positioning the Smaller Pot: Carefully place the smaller terracotta pot upside down over the support structure so that it's elevated above the candles. Ensure it's centered and the hole at the bottom (now at the top) is unobstructed for airflow.

Adding the Larger Pot: Now, take your larger pot and place it over the smaller one, again making sure it's upside down and the hole at the top is clear. The smaller pot should fit snugly inside the larger one, creating an effective heat chamber. Ensure that both pots are stable on the support structure.

Optional Coin Cover: Some people like to place a coin over the hole of the inner pot to help retain more heat. This is optional and should be done carefully to avoid blocking too much airflow.

Step 3: Maintaining optimal heat

Give it Time: It'll take a few minutes for your heater to reach its full potential. As it warms up, you'll feel the pots becoming hot to the touch.

Heat Distribution: For the best results, position your heater in the part of the room where you'd like more warmth. Remember, this is a spot heater, so it's perfect for personal use or heating a small area.

Adjusting as Needed: Depending on the heat output, you might want to adjust the number of candles or even the arrangement. Feel free to experiment to find what works best for your space.

Step 4: Safety checks and precautions

Never Leave It Unattended: This can't be stressed enough. Never leave your candle heater unattended. Always extinguish the candles if you're leaving the room or going to sleep.

Surface Checks: Regularly ensure that the base under your heater hasn't become too hot. If it has, you might need to improve your base to better insulate the heat.

Ventilation: Make sure the room is well-ventilated. While candles don't produce a ton of carbon monoxide, any flame eats up oxygen and produces some amount of gas. A little fresh air goes a long way in keeping things safe.

Extinguishing: When you're done using the heater or if any of the candles have burned out, carefully extinguish the remaining candles. Let the pots cool down completely before handling them, as they can retain heat for quite a while.

Maximizing Efficiency and Usage

To get the most out of your candle heater, consider where and how long you use it. Placing it in a smaller room or near the area you're sitting can maximize its warming effect. Use it for shorter periods to enjoy a cozy atmosphere and remember, it's best for supplemental heat, not as your primary source.

Long-burning candles are your friends here. Opt for those with a longer life to extend your heating sessions without constant replacements. Also, arranging your candles so each one gets enough oxygen and burns efficiently can make a difference.

For an even heat distribution, make sure the pots are centered and the air can circulate well around them. Occasionally rotating the heater can also help spread the warmth more uniformly across the room.

Creative Variations and Decor

Your candle powered heater doesn't just have to be functional; it can be a piece of art! Feel free to paint the terracotta pots with heat-resistant paint or add designs to reflect your personal style. Just ensure whatever you use is safe for high temperatures.

Incorporating your heater into your home decor can make it an interesting conversation piece. Place it on a decorative stand or surround it with non-flammable decorations to blend it seamlessly into your space, adding both warmth and style.

And there you have it! With these tips, you should have a charming, functional candle-powered heater adding a bit of extra warmth to your space. Enjoy the cozy vibes, and remember to always prioritize safety in your off-grid adventures.

2

CAPTURING DAYLIGHT WITH BOTTLES

TURN BOTTLES INTO LIGHT BULBS BY DIFFUSING
SUNLIGHT INTO DARK ROOM

In this chapter, we're going to explore a simple yet ingenious method that's lighting up lives in areas where the luxury of electricity isn't a given. Imagine turning everyday plastic bottles into a source of light, bright enough to rival a 40-60 watt bulb. It's a game-changer for many, and it could be an enlightening experiment for you too.

This technique is as straightforward as it is brilliant. With just a clear plastic bottle, some water, and a bit of bleach, people in underserved communities are diffusing sunlight into their homes, turning dimly lit rooms into spaces filled with a soft, ambient glow.

We'll delve into how this method works, why it's so effective, and how you can create your own bottle light. Whether you're looking to reduce your carbon footprint, tackle a fun project, or simply curious about sustainable living practices around the world, there's something in here for you. So, let's start this enlightening journey together.

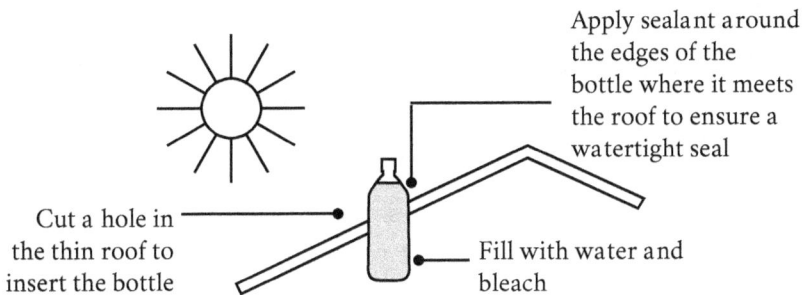

Apply sealant around the edges of the bottle where it meets the roof to ensure a watertight seal

Cut a hole in the thin roof to insert the bottle

Fill with water and bleach

How Does It Work?

How sunlight is diffused through the bottle

The concept of turning a bottle into a light source is very simple. It begins with taking a clear plastic bottle, filling it with water, and adding a small amount of bleach. The bottle is then fixed into a hole in the roof, with part of it outside under the sun and the other half inside a dark room.

When sunlight hits the bottle, something happens - the light bends. This bending is called "refraction," and it's the same trick that makes a straw look broken in a glass of water. In our bottle, this bending spreads the sunlight out in all directions inside the room instead of just one straight line. This way, the bottle acts like a light bulb, glowing and illuminating the space around it.

The bleach in the water isn't just for show; it keeps the water clean and clear. This means no algae or other things clouding up the bottle. We want the light as bright as possible, and clean water is key to that.

How the bottle light is set up

Setting up a bottle light is surprisingly easy. Here's a quick run-down:

1. Clear Plastic Bottle: A standard 1-1.5 liter bottle, typically used for soft drinks, is ideal. The bottle must be clear to allow as much light as possible to pass through.

2. Water: Water fills the bottle, serving as the medium that allows sunlight to be refracted and diffused.

3. Bleach: A small amount is added to the water to keep it clear by preventing algae from growing inside the bottle.

4. Secure Roof: The roof must be suitable for cutting a hole to fit the bottle. It should be thin enough to work with, but sturdy enough to support the bottle without collapsing.

By using these readily available materials, people in areas with limited resources can create a daylight source for their rooms. It's a sustainable, cost-effective solution that's easy to make. And the best part is that it harnesses the sun, an endless energy source available during the day.

What Works and What Doesn't

Here we'll explore the key factors that make this method shine and the limitations you should be aware of. It's all about knowing what to expect and how to make the most of it.

Key factors for this to work

There are two key factors for bottle lights to work: the intensity of sunlight and the darkness of the space. The amount of light your bottle emits is proportional to the intensity of sunlight it catches. The brighter and more direct the sunlight, the more effective your bottle light will be. This is why bottle lights are a hit in areas close to the equator or those with long, sunny days.

Equally important is the darkness of the room. The contrast created by a very dark room enhances the effect of the diffused light, making the room feel much brighter. So, the best candidates for bottle lights are those dimly lit corners or windowless rooms.

Limitations

Reliance on Abundant Sunlight: The biggest limitation is perhaps the most obvious one — you need sunshine, and plenty of it. On cloudy days, during heavy rain, or in the long winter months, the effectiveness of the bottle light will naturally decrease. This reliance on sunny weather means that bottle lights are more suited to certain climates than others.

Installation Requirements: To get your bottle light up and running, you'll need to cut a hole in the roof or walls. This might not be feasible for everyone. It requires a bit of DIY know-how, and you'll want to ensure that it's done safely and securely to avoid leaks or damage.

Daytime Only: Bottle lights are fantastic during the day, but as the sun sets, so does their magic. They don't store or emit light after dark, so you'll need an alternative light source for the night. This makes them a great supplement to traditional lighting but not a complete replacement.

Maintenance Required: To keep your bottle light at its best, regular maintenance is key. This includes cleaning the outside to remove any dust or debris and ensuring the water inside remains clear. If the water gets cloudy or the bleach loses its effectiveness, it's time for a refresh. Neglecting maintenance can greatly reduce the effectiveness of bottle light.

Durability of Bottles: It's important to consider the durability of bottle lights. Plastic bottles, especially when exposed to constant sunlight, aren't the most durable material. Over time, they can degrade, become brittle, or even warp, which can lead to breakages. In extreme weather conditions, they might not hold up well, leading to a need for replacements or repairs.

In conclusion, while bottle lights are a clever and sustainable way to brighten up dark spaces, they come with their own set of considerations. By understanding these key factors and limitations, you can better prepare and decide if this is the right solution for you.

Materials and Tools Needed

Before you begin, ensure you have all the necessary materials and tools:

Plastic Bottles (1-1.5 liter): Opt for clear and colorless for the best results. PET soda bottles are the best options.

Water (1-1.5 liter): Just your regular tap water will do. It's going to fill up those bottles.

Bleach: A splash (2 tsp.) of household liquid Chlorine bleach in the water keeps things clear.

Silicone Sealant: Use this when you install the bottle to ensure a watertight seal.

Tools: A cutter or a saw to make the hole for your bottle, and some gloves and safety glasses for safety. You'll also want a measuring tape to make sure everything lines up right.

Step-by-Step Guide

Step 1: Preparing the Bottle with Water and Bleach

Clean the bottle thoroughly, make sure it's free from labels, dirt, and any residue. The clearer the bottle, the better the light diffusion.

Fill the bottle with 1-1.5 liter of clean water.

Add 2 tsp. of liquid bleach to the water. This will prevent algae growth and keep the water clear for longer.

Close the bottle tightly with its cap to avoid any spillage.

Step 2: Cutting a Hole in the Roof and Ensuring It's the Right Size

Determine the location on the roof where the bottle light will be most effective. It should be a dark area during the day that receives direct sunlight.

Use a measuring tape to mark the diameter of the bottle on the roof. The hole should be slightly smaller (1/16 inches) than the bottle's diameter to ensure a snug fit.

Cut the hole using the tools. Exercise caution and wear gloves and safety glasses for protection.

Clean the hole to make sure there are no sharp or rough edges.

Step 3: Inserting and Securing the Bottle

Insert the bottle into the hole. At least one-third of the bottle should protrude from the top of the roof.

Ensure that the bottle fits snugly into the hole. If necessary, adjust until you achieve a tight fit.

Once in place, use a waterproof sealant around the bottle's edges where it meets the roof. This will prevent any water leaks during rain and ensure the bottle remains secure.

Remember, always prioritize safety while working at heights or with tools.

Maximizing Efficiency and Light Output

For the bottle light to work effectively, it's essential to optimize its placement. Here are some tips for maximizing the light output.

Best Placement for the Bottles

Direct Sunlight: Place the bottle in a place that receives direct sunlight for most of the day. The more sunlight the bottle receives, the brighter the light will be. North or south-facing directions might work best depending on your hemisphere.

Dark Areas: Target the installation to the darkest areas of the room. The contrast between the bright light from the bottle and the dark environment will make the bottle light more effective.

Even Distribution: If installing multiple bottle lights, space them evenly to ensure an even distribution of light throughout the room.

Height Consideration: Install the bottle at the highest point of the room to allow the light to disperse downwards and cover a wider area.

Maintaining Light's Efficiency Over Time

Regular Cleaning: Keep the exterior part of the bottle clean from dust and dirt. A dirty bottle can greatly diminish the light's intensity. Clean it regularly with water and a gentle cleaning agent.

Water and Bleach Replacement: Over time, the water inside the bottle may become cloudy or the bleach may become less effective. Refresh the water and bleach mixture as needed, to ensure the light remains clear and bright.

Check for Algae: Even with bleach, algae or other organisms might grow, especially in warmer climates. Regularly inspect the bottle for signs of growth and replace the solution if necessary.

Sealant Inspection: Periodically check the sealant around the bottle for any cracks or signs of wear. A well-sealed bottle prevents leaks and ensures no water gets into the home during rainy seasons.

Avoid Shading: Ensure that new constructions, trees, or installations around the home don't start shading the bottle over time. The bottle should remain free from any shade to be effective.

The Movement Behind

Let's take a moment to tip our hats to the guy who started it all: Alfredo Moser. Back in 2002, during one of the frequent blackouts in his Brazilian hometown, Moser had a lightbulb moment—literally. He filled up plastic bottles with water and bleach, and used them to light up his workshop. Simple, but genius! His idea spread like wildfire, and soon, people everywhere were lighting up their homes using his method.

Fast forward to the Liter of Light movement, kicked off by Illac Diaz. This initiative took Moser's idea global, bringing sustain-

21

able lighting to underprivileged communities worldwide. It's all about empowerment, teaching people to use simple materials to brighten their lives. The movement has lit up hundreds and thousands of homes, and you can find out more on their website literoflight.org.

The movement didn't stop at just daytime lighting. They've tweaked to create versions that work at night too, using small solar panels and batteries to store energy during the day and keep the light shining when the sun sets.

3

NATURE'S FRIDGE OF THE EGYPTIANS

USE A ZEER POT (POT-IN-POT FRIDGE) TO KEEP
THINGS COOL WITHOUT ELECTRICITY

The zeer pot, an ancient method revived for modern times, offers a way to keep things cool without electricity. The concept dates back to the ancient Egyptians, who used porous clay pots for cooling. Then, in the 1990s, Mohammed Bah Abba, a teacher from Nigeria, modernized this ancient technique, creating the zeer pot as we know it today for food preservation. So, if you're ready to embrace a greener way of living, the zeer pot is your ally in the quest for natural refrigeration.

How Does It Work?

The zeer pot is made of two terracotta pots, one smaller than the other. The smaller pot sits inside the larger one, and the space in between is filled with wet sand. The top is covered with a wet cloth.

The zeer pot works on the principle of evaporative cooling.

When water in the sand evaporates, it takes heat from the inner pot, lowering the temperature inside. This can keep the contents several degrees cooler than the surrounding environment, perfect for storing perishables like fruits, vegetables, and even some types of dairy.

However, the zeer pot isn't a one-size-fits-all solution. Its effectiveness depends on the climate — it works best in dry, arid conditions where evaporation happens faster. And while it won't replace your electric fridge for all needs, it offers a sustainable solution for reducing reliance on energy.

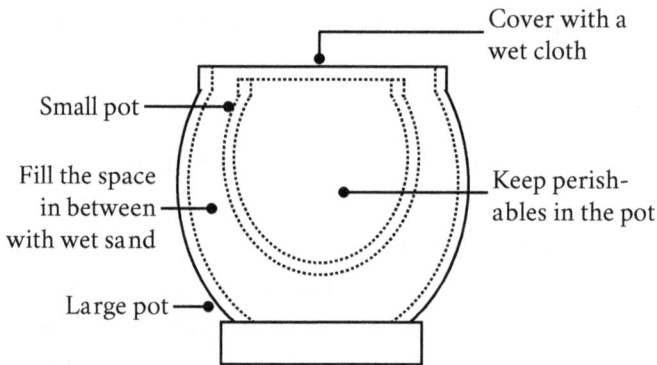

Cover with a wet cloth

Small pot

Fill the space in between with wet sand

Keep perishables in the pot

Large pot

Building Your Own Fridge

Materials Needed and Where to Find Them

The beauty of the zeer pot is in its simplicity. Here's the materials needed for the project:

Terracotta Pots: You'll need two terracotta pots, one smaller than the other so it can fit inside with some room to spare. Look for these at garden centers or home improvement stores. Make sure one is slightly larger than the other.

Sand: Fine, clean sand works best. You might find it at a building supply store or a craft shop.

Cloth or Burlap: You'll also need a piece of cloth or burlap large enough to cover the top. Old t-shirts, towels, or any fabric that retains moisture will do. Burlap is often used for its durability and airflow properties.

Water: Just plain, clean water.

Step-by-step Guide on Making a Basic Zeer Pot

Here's how you can create the zeer pot with a few simple materials:

1. Prepare the Pots: Make sure the inner surface of your pots is clean and dry. If there are any holes in the bottom of the pots, plug them up with some clay or silicone sealant. You want to ensure the water stays in the sand, not seeping out the bottom.

2. Place the Smaller Pot Inside the Larger One: Now, nestle the smaller pot inside the larger one. The space between them is where the magic happens.

3. Fill the Gap with Sand: Pour clean, fine sand into the gap between the pots until it reaches about an inch from the top. The sand acts as a wick, drawing water up and allowing it to evaporate, which cools the inner pot.

4. Moisten the Sand: Slowly add water to the sand until it's visibly wet, but not waterlogged. You want the sand to be damp all around because it's this moisture that will evaporate and do the cooling.

5. Cover the Top: Use a wet cloth or a piece of burlap to cover the top of the inner pot. This helps maintain the humidity inside and maximizes the cooling effect.

6. Place in a Dry, Breezy Spot: Find a spot with good airflow and some shade for your zeer pot. Air movement enhances the evaporation process, and keeping it out of direct sunlight prevents the water from heating up too quickly.

Maximizing Efficiency

Placement

The location of your zeer pot can significantly affect its performance. For maximum cooling, place it in a dry, well-ventilated area. Air movement is crucial as it speeds up evaporation, so consider spots with natural breezes or where air circulates well. Avoid direct sunlight, as it can heat the pot and counteract the cooling effect. If you're in a humid climate, the zeer pot may be less effective, as the air can't take on as much moisture, slowing down the evaporation process.

Pre-Cooling and Patience

For best results, don't put hot items directly into the zeer pot. Let them cool to room temperature first. Moreover, patience is key when using a zeer pot. Unlike the rapid cooling effect of a modern fridge, the zeer pot cools contents gradually. The process relies on the steady evaporation of water, which lowers the temperature inside.

How to Maintain and Clean Your Zeer Pot

Maintenance is key to the longevity of your zeer pot. Regularly refill the water to keep the sand moist. Monitor the inner pot for any signs of mold or algae and clean both pots with a brush and some mild soap if you notice any growth. Allow these pots to dry completely in the sun before reassembling. Refresh the sand periodically, as it can become compacted or dirty over time, which can impede its wicking abilities.

Common Problems and Solutions

One issue might be insufficient cooling. If this happens, ensure that the pot is in an optimal location and that the sand and cloth are adequately moist. If the air is too humid, the evaporation process slows down, reducing the cooling effect. In this case, finding a drier area or increasing air circulation can help. Cracks or damage to the pots can also hinder performance, so handle them with care and inspect them regularly for any signs of wear.

Creative Uses

Different Ways to Utilize the Zeer Pot Beyond Just Cooling Food

Beyond just keeping your vegetables crisp and dairy fresh, the zeer pot can have other uses. You can use it to cool drinking water or even as a makeshift cellar for storing seeds or nuts. Some have used smaller versions to keep medications cool in areas without electricity. The zeer pot's cooling effect can also create a more comfortable microclimate, so placing it near your sitting area can help cool you down on hot days.

Variations of the Design for Different Climates and Needs

While the traditional zeer pot works best in dry, arid climates, variations have been adapted for more humid environments. Some people add a third pot or use insulating materials to enhance the cooling effect. Others have experimented with different types of sand or even using alternative materials like rice husks. Innovators have also attached small fans to increase air circulation around the pot, further enhancing the cooling effect. These variations showcase the versatility of the zeer pot, making it a customizable tool for sustainable living worldwide.

Real-Life Success Stories

In Nigeria, a woman entrepreneur revolutionized her village's food storage with the zeer pot, greatly reducing spoilage and sustaining her community's food supply. In arid regions, families have reported that vegetables and fruits last weeks longer, transforming their diets and reducing waste. Zeer pot is not just a tool, but a life-enhancing solution, providing food security and fostering independence in areas hit hardest by the lack of refrigeration.

Limitations

While zeer pots are beneficial, they have limitations. The size can also limit the amount of food stored, and they require daily maintenance to ensure optimal performance. Additionally, while they reduce temperatures significantly, they do not reach the low temperatures of modern fridge, which may be necessary for some perishables. Understanding and adapting to these limitations is crucial for anyone looking to incorporate zeer pots into their lifestyle effectively.

4

POTENT CLEANERS, MINIMAL COST

MAKE CLEANING SOLUTIONS FROM VINEGAR, BAKING SODA, AND LEMON

Ever looked at the ingredients list on a bottle of cleaner and felt like you needed a chemistry degree to understand it? Welcome the world of natural cleaning products, where vinegar, baking soda, and lemon take center stage. These aren't just staple foods in your kitchen; they're also your allies in keeping your home spotless and fresh.

Vinegar, with its natural acidity, is a whiz at breaking down grease and banishing bad smells. Baking soda is a gentle abrasive that's perfect for scrubbing away stubborn spots while neutralizing odors. And lemons are not just for lemonade. Their citric acid and fresh scent make them powerful stain fighters and natural fresheners. Together, they form a cleaning product that tackles everything from grimy countertops to dull floors. Let's get ready to turn these kitchen staples into your new favorite cleaning agents.

Why Go Natural?

Why reach for the bottle of harsh chemicals when a safer, more environmentally friendly solution is sitting right in your pantry? Going natural with your cleaning isn't just a trend; it's a healthier choice for you. Those conventional cleaners often come packed with ingredients that can irritate your eyes and respiratory system. Switching to natural alternatives can greatly reduce these health risks.

And think about the environment. Every time you rinse a chemical cleaner down the drain, it embarks on a journey through our waterways, potentially impacting aquatic life and ecosystems. Natural cleaners, on the other hand, are biodegradable and far less damaging.

But here's the real kicker: using natural cleaners can also be kinder to your wallet. These ingredients are cost-effective, widely available, and incredibly versatile. So, by going natural, you're not just making a healthy and eco-friendly choice, you're also opting for a more economical way to keep your home sparkling. Now, isn't that something worth considering as you wield your spray bottle and scrub brush?

Getting Started with Basics

Now that you're all set to switch up your cleaning routine, let's understand the cleaning trio better: vinegar, baking soda, and lemon. Each of these ingredients has unique properties that make them household cleaning champions.

Distilled White Vinegar: This kitchen staple is essentially diluted acetic acid, which makes it terrific at cutting through grease and grime. It's also a natural deodorizer and can kill some bacteria and viruses, making it a go-to for many cleaning tasks. However, its acidic nature means it's not suitable for use on natural stone or certain delicate surfaces, as it can etch or dull them.

Baking Soda: Known chemically as sodium bicarbonate, baking soda is a mild alkali, which makes it great at dissolving dirt and grease in water. Its abrasive texture helps with scrubbing tasks, and it's a natural deodorizer too. Plus, it's safe for almost all surfaces, making it incredibly versatile.

Lemon: The high concentration of citric acid in lemons gives them their natural antibacterial and antiseptic properties. They're great for cutting through tough stains, especially on surfaces like cutting boards and countertops. Plus, that fresh citrus scent leaves everything smelling clean.

When storing these ingredients, keep vinegar in its original bottle in a cool, dark place. Baking soda should be kept in a dry, sealed container to prevent it from clumping or reacting with any moisture. Lemons are best kept in your fridge's crisper drawer where they'll stay fresh longer.

Remember, while these ingredients are natural, they're still potent. As with any cleaning product, natural or not, it's wise to do a small patch test on surfaces before going all in, just to be safe.

Recipes for Every Room

Here's a collection of recipes tailored for various rooms and purposes, using our trio of vinegar, baking soda, and lemon.

Kitchen Cleaners

All-purpose cleaner

Combine 1 part water with 1 part distilled white vinegar in a spray bottle. If you love a fresh scent, add a few drops of your favorite essential oil or some lemon peels. This solution works wonders on countertops, appliances, and kitchen tables. Just spray, wipe with a cloth, and revel in the clean.

Grease cutter

For those stubborn greasy surfaces, mix 2 parts baking soda with 1 part lemon juice to form a paste. Apply it to the greasy area and let it sit for a few minutes before scrubbing off. The abrasive baking soda combined with the grease-cutting power of lemon works miracles on even the grimiest surfaces.

Microwave and oven cleaner

Say goodbye to microwave splatters and oven grime. In a microwave-safe bowl, mix 2 tablespoons of baking soda, 1 cup water, and a few slices of lemon. Microwave for about 3 minutes or until it boils and steams. Let it cool for a moment, then wipe down the inside with a sponge. The steam loosens the grime, and the lemon deodorizes, leaving you with a sparkling clean appliance.

Bathroom Boosters

Grout cleaner

For dingy grout, mix 3 parts baking soda with 1 part water to create a paste. Apply this to the grout, and then spray with vinegar. The mixture will foam up, breaking down the dirt and mildew. Scrub with a brush and rinse for a pristine finish.

Toilet bowl cleaner

Add one cup of vinegar to the toilet bowl and allow it sit for several minutes. Next, sprinkle baking soda around the interior of the bowl. Use a toilet brush to scrub thoroughly. The mixture of vinegar and baking soda effectively cleans and freshens your toilet, all without the need for strong chemicals.

Shower spray

Keep a spray bottle filled with a mixture of equal parts vinegar and water in your bathroom. After showering, spritz the walls and curtain or door to prevent mildew and soap scum buildup. For extra antibacterial power and a pleasant scent, add a few drops of tea tree or eucalyptus essential oil.

Living Spaces

Window and glass cleaner

Mix 2 cups of water, 1/2 cup vinegar, and a 1/4 cup of rubbing alcohol with a squirt of liquid dish soap in a spray bottle. This concoction will leave your windows and mirrors gleaming without any streaks. Just spray, wipe with a lint-free cloth or newspaper, and admire the clarity you've created!

Advanced Tips and Tricks

When your standard natural cleaning solutions need a little extra oomph, consider these advanced tips and tricks. For tougher stains or dirt, create a more potent paste with baking soda and a smaller amount of water, then add a few drops of lemon juice for extra stain-fighting power. Apply it to the affected area, let it sit, then scrub away.

During spring cleaning, or any seasonal deep-clean, amplify your natural solutions with fresh, seasonal herbs. For instance, in spring and summer, add fresh mint or lavender to your mixes for a refreshing, antimicrobial boost. In the fall, cinnamon or clove can provide warming and antiseptic properties.

Surfaces to Avoid

While vinegar, baking soda, and lemon are versatile and effective for many cleaning tasks, there are certain surfaces and materials where their use is not recommended.

1. Natural Stone Surfaces: Surfaces like granite, marble, and limestone are sensitive to acidic substances. Vinegar and lemon, due to their acidity, can etch and dull these surfaces. For cleaning natural stone, it's best to use mild, pH-neutral cleaners.

2. Hardwood Floors: While some hardwood floors can handle diluted vinegar solutions, it's generally advised to avoid using vinegar or lemon juice. These acidic substances can degrade the finish over time, leading to dullness and damage. Instead, use a cleaner formulated for hardwood.

3. Waxed Furniture and Floors: Vinegar or lemon can strip away the wax coating on waxed furniture and floors, leading to a loss of shine and protection. Use a soap-based cleaner that's safe for waxed surfaces.

4. Aluminum and Stainless Steel: Acidic cleaners can cause discoloration and damage to aluminum surfaces and some stainless steel. It's safer to use a mild detergent and water for these materials.

5. Electronic Screens: Avoid using vinegar or lemon-based cleaners on screens of TVs, computers, and smartphones. The acidity can damage the anti-glare properties and may even remove the screen's protective coating. Use a microfiber cloth and a cleaner designed for electronics.

6. Egg Stains or Spills: When dealing with egg spills or stains, avoid using hot water or acidic cleaners like vinegar. They can coagulate the egg protein, making it harder to remove. Opt for cold water and a mild detergent instead.

7. Pet Messes: For cleaning pet urine, avoid vinegar as it can amplify the urine odor. Enzymatic cleaners are more effective for neutralizing these odors and removing stains.

Remember, natural doesn't always mean safe for every surface. When in doubt, test a small area first for the appropriate cleaning method.

Safety and Precautions

While natural, ingredients like vinegar and baking soda are potent and should be used wisely. Never mix vinegar with bleach, as it creates harmful chlorine gas. Also, be cautious when combining vinegar and hydrogen peroxide, as it can form a corrosive acid. Always store your homemade cleaners in clearly labeled containers, out of reach of children and pets. Even natural cleaners can be harmful if ingested or used improperly.

Personalizing Your Cleaning Solutions

Make cleaning more enjoyable by personalizing your solutions. Add a few drops of your favorite essential oils like lavender, lemon, or eucalyptus to any mix for a customized fragrance that also offers additional antibacterial or antifungal properties. Get creative with labels and storage, using glass spray bottles and custom labels. Not only will your home be clean and fresh, but it'll also feel more 'you'. Plus, these personalized bottles make thoughtful, eco-friendly gifts for friends and family looking to start their natural cleaning journey.

5

CLIMATE STABILIZERS WITH WATER

USE BARRELS OF WATER TO ABSORB AND
REDISTRIBUTE HEAT IN A GREENHOUSE

In the world of greenhouse gardening, maintaining a consistent temperature is crucial for plant health and growth. That's where water barrels come in, not as a source of water, but as a powerful tool to stabilize the temperature within your greenhouse. This method isn't just about keeping your plants happy. It's a sustainable approach to temperature control, reducing the need for electrical heating systems and minimizing energy consumption. Plus, it's relatively simple and cost-effective to implement. With a few well-placed barrels and some sunshine, you can create a more stable growing environment for a wide variety of plants.

Greenhouse Climate Control

Integrating heat sinks like water barrels into your greenhouse is a game-changer for temperature control. So, what's the magic behind this method? It's all about the thermal mass properties of water. Water has the ability to absorb, store, and later release large amounts of heat. By placing barrels of water in your greenhouse, you're creating large batteries of heat that absorb excess warmth when the sun is shining and release it slowly when the temperatures drop, particularly during the cool nights. This not only helps protect your plants but also can extend your growing season by keeping temperatures more stable. Heat sinks are a passive, energy-efficient solution to one of the most significant challenges in greenhouse gardening: maintaining an optimal growing climate. With the right setup, they can greatly reduce the energy consumption and costs associated with active heating and cooling systems.

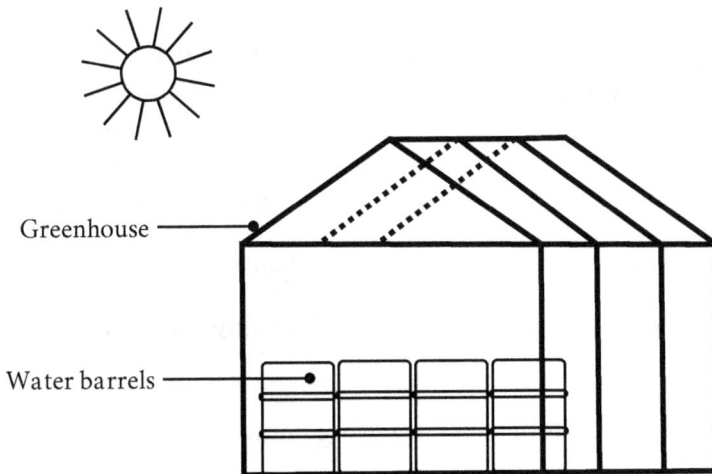

Materials and Tools Needed

To set up an effective water barrel heat sink system in your greenhouse, you'll need the right materials and tools. Here's what to gather:

Types of Barrels Suitable for Use

Plastic Barrels: Often used due to their durability, light weight, and resistance to rot. Look for food-grade barrels if possible, as they ensure the water doesn't get contaminated with harmful substances.

Metal Barrels: These can also be used but ensure they are coated to prevent rusting. They're heavier but have high thermal conductivity.

Other Materials Needed

Black Paint (non-toxic): Painting your barrels black will increase their heat absorption capability as black absorbs more heat.

Pipe or Hose: Needed if you plan to integrate the barrel with a watering system or for easier filling and draining.

Insulation Material (optional): To wrap around the barrels to reduce heat loss, especially useful in very cold climates.

Tools Required for Assembly and Setup:

Drill: For making holes if you're attaching pipes or creating an integrated watering system.

Paintbrush or Roller: For applying paint to the barrels.

Gloves and Safety Goggles: Always prioritize safety when handling tools and materials.

Selection and Preparation

Selecting the Right Barrel Size

When choosing barrels for your greenhouse, consider the size and material. The size will depend on the available space and the amount of heat you need to absorb. Typically, 55-gallon drums are used, but the number and size can vary based on your specific needs. Ensure the barrels haven't previously stored harmful chemicals, especially if they'll be in close proximity to plants or water systems.

Cleaning and Preparing Barrels

Cleaning: Thoroughly clean the barrels with a mixture of water and a non-toxic cleaner. Rinse well to ensure no residues remain.

Painting: Paint the barrels black to maximize heat absorption. Use several coats of non-toxic, water-resistant paint suitable for the barrel's material.

Inspection: Check for any leaks or weak spots, especially if using second-hand barrels.

Installation Process

Now that you've got your materials prepared and your barrels ready, it's time to install them in your greenhouse and get ready to harness the thermal power of water. Follow this step-by-step guide to ensure a smooth installation:

1. Positioning Your Barrels

Sunlight Maximization: Place your barrels in a location where they will receive maximum sunlight throughout the day. Typically, this is against the north wall if you live in the north hemisphere or under the highest point of the greenhouse roof.

Spacing: Leave enough space between the barrels and other objects or walls to allow for air circulation, which helps with more even heat distribution.

2. Securing the Barrels

Stability is Key: Ensure each barrel is stable and won't roll or tip. You might want to place them on a platform or secure them with straps or weights, especially if you're in an area prone to movement or strong winds.

Fill with Water: Once the barrels are in place and stable, fill them with water. This can be done with a hose or buckets, depending on your setup and water source.

3. Maximizing Heat Absorption

Orientation: If possible, orient the barrels so the largest surface area faces the sun's path. This depends on the greenhouse's design and the sun's trajectory.

Color Matters: If you haven't already, ensure the barrels are painted black or a dark color to absorb more heat during the day.

4. Enhancing Heat Distribution

Use of Reflective Surfaces: Consider placing reflective materials like aluminum foil or reflective fabric behind the barrels to bounce back any escaping heat towards the plants.

Air Circulation: Strategically use fans or vents to help distribute the warm air from around the barrels throughout the greenhouse.

5. Safety Measures

Weight Support: Remember, water is heavy. Ensure that the greenhouse structure and the platform holding the barrels can support the weight when they are full.

Regular Inspection: Periodically check the barrels for leaks or any signs of wear and tear. Resolve any problems right away to avoid water damage and maintain optimal efficiency.

Emergency Plan: Have a plan for quickly draining the barrels if needed, whether due to a leak or structural concern. Know how you will remove or replace a barrel if it becomes necessary.

Maintenance and Monitoring

Routine Checks and Cleaning

Regularly inspect your barrels for any signs of algae growth, sediment buildup, or leaks. Clean the exterior surfaces to ensure they continue to absorb maximum sunlight. If needed, empty the barrels periodically for a thorough interior cleaning, especially if the water becomes cloudy or discolored.

Monitoring Temperature Changes

Keep a close eye on the temperature inside your greenhouse, especially during extreme weather conditions. Use a minimum-maximum thermometer to track the range of temperatures throughout the day and night.

Adjust the positioning of the barrels or the amount of water as seasons change. In warmer months, you might need less water to prevent overheating, while in cooler months, you might fill them up to maximize heat absorption.

Troubleshooting Common Issues

If you notice the temperature isn't being regulated as effectively, first ensure the barrels are properly filled and haven't developed leaks. Check that they're still in the optimal position for sunlight exposure and haven't been shaded by new plant growth or structural changes in the greenhouse. If algae growth is an issue, consider covering the barrels to limit light penetration or adding a small amount of non-toxic algaecide. Regularly revisiting and fine-tuning your setup is key to maintaining an effective heat sink system.

Maximizing Efficiency

To enhance the performance of your water barrel system, consider the following tips:

Insulate your greenhouse to retain more of the heat absorbed during the day.

Pair your water barrel system with other passive solar features, like a south-facing wall painted black, to increase heat absorption.

During colder months, add more barrels if space allows to increase the total heat storage capacity.

Keep the water level as high as possible in each barrel to maximize thermal mass.

By following these steps, you'll set up an efficient, sustainable heating system that leverages the natural power of water and sunlight. Not only will your plants benefit from the more stable temperatures, but you'll also enjoy the peace of mind that comes from a well-maintained, eco-friendly solution.

6

LIFESAVING, EASIEST WATER PURIFICATION

DISINFECT WATER USING SOLAR RADIATION IN
CLEAR PLASTIC BOTTLES

Solar Water Disinfection (SODIS) is a game-changer; it uses solar energy to disinfect water, making it safe to drink. This process is particularly useful in areas where access to clean water is a challenge. Simply put, SODIS involves filling plastic bottles with water and exposing them to the sun for several hours or days. The solar radiation and heat work together to kill harmful pathogens in the water, making it safe to drink.

The concept might sound modern, but it's been around for ages, with historical records indicating various methods of solar water treatment. Today, SODIS is celebrated as an accessible, cost-effective solution, especially in developing countries. It requires minimal equipment and no electricity.

How Does It Work?

The effectiveness of SODIS lies in the dual power of UV radiation and increased temperature.

UV Radiation: The sun emits ultraviolet (UV) rays, which are a type of electromagnetic radiation. When harmful microorganisms in the water are exposed to UV rays, the radiation penetrates their cells and damages their DNA.

Temperature: Simultaneously, the sun's heat increases the water's temperature. When combined with UV exposure, higher temperatures accelerate the disinfection process. Ideally, the water should reach at least 50°C (122°F) for enhanced effectiveness, though lower temperatures still benefit from UV exposure.

The best part? This process doesn't require any sophisticated technology or chemicals. Clear plastic bottles are usually made from PET, which allows most of the UV rays to pass through and doesn't leach harmful substances into the water. By laying bottles out in direct sunlight, typically for about six hours or up to two days if the sky is overcast, you can significantly reduce the presence of pathogens.

Materials and Setup

To embark on your solar disinfection journey, you'll need the right materials and a bit of know-how for setting everything up. Here's what you need to know:

Types of Bottles Suitable for SODIS

The ideal bottles for SODIS are clear plastic PET bottles. PET bottles allow UV rays to penetrate the water effectively. They are commonly used for beverages and are readily available.

Use bottles that are between 1-2 liters in capacity for the best results. Larger bottles may not allow UV rays to penetrate to the center of the water volume effectively.

Ensure the bottles are transparent and not colored, as clear bottles maximize UV light penetration. Avoid using cloudy plastics as they can impede UV exposure.

Preparing the Water and Bottles for Disinfection

Start by cleaning the bottles thoroughly with soap and water. If a bottle has been used previously, ensure it's free from any residues or dirt.

Fill the bottles with water. If the water is turbid or cloudy, it needs to be filtered or settled first. Clear water allows UV rays to penetrate more effectively.

Do not fill the bottle to the brim; leave a little space to allow for expansion when the water heats and to shake the bottle to oxygenate the water, enhancing the effectiveness of the process.

Setting Up Your SODIS Station

Location: Choose a sunny spot where the bottles will receive maximum sunlight. This could be a flat roof, a yard, or a balcony. Avoid shaded areas as they can significantly slow down the disinfection process.

Orientation: Lay the bottles down horizontally to maximize the surface area exposed to the sun. This orientation helps the UV rays penetrate through more of the water.

Duration: The required exposure time can vary from 6 hours to two days, depending on weather conditions and the intensity of the sunlight. On bright, sunny days, 6 hours is typically sufficient. However, on cloudy days or when the water temperature is cooler, it might take two days for effective disinfection.

The setup for SODIS is straightforward but requires attention to detail to ensure the process is effective. With your bottles prepped and your station set, you're ready to harness the power of the sun for water disinfection.

Best Practices

SODIS is a straightforward yet nuanced process. To ensure its effectiveness, here are some best practices you should follow:

Ensuring Water Clarity and Optimal Conditions for Disinfection

Water Clarity: The clearer the water, the better. Cloudy or turbid water reduces the penetration of UV rays and makes SODIS less effective. Use a cloth or a coffee filter to pre-filter water if it's not clear.

Aeration: Before sealing the bottles, shake them for about 20 seconds to oxygenate the water. This aeration helps enhance the disinfection process.

Maintenance of Bottles: Regularly inspect your bottles for scratches, cloudiness, or any signs of wear. Damaged or old bottles might impede UV transmission and should be replaced.

Frequency and Timing of Water Treatment

Daily Treatment: In continuous use, treat water daily to ensure a steady supply of safe drinking water. It's a good practice to set up a rotation system where some bottles are being disinfected while others are ready for use.

Timing: Start the SODIS process in the morning to utilize the maximum hours of sunlight. Ensure the bottles are exposed during peak sun hours (usually between 10 am to 3 pm).

How to Tell When the Water is Safe to Drink

Duration: Generally, if the water has been exposed to full sunlight for at least 6 hours or two days of 50% cloud cover, it's safe. However, this can vary based on the intensity of the sun and the ambient temperature.

Temperature: If the bottles feel warm or hot to the touch, it's a good sign that they've received enough heat and UV exposure. Water temperatures above 50°C combined with UV exposure enhance the disinfection process.

Indicator Tools: Some organizations provide indicators or use methods like WADI, a UV measurement tool, to indicate when water has been sufficiently exposed to UV rays. These can be helpful if you're unsure about the sun's intensity or the water's safety.

Remember, while SODIS is a robust method for disinfection, if you ever doubt the safety of the treated water or if conditions haven't been ideal, it's prudent to err on the side of caution and treat the water for a bit longer or use an alternative method to ensure its safety.

Benefits and Limitations

Benefits of SODIS

Cost-Effective: SODIS requires minimal investment, mostly in the form of plastic bottles, which are often readily available and inexpensive.

Simple and Accessible: The process is straightforward and can be easily adopted by individuals and communities alike, without the need for extensive training or complex equipment.

Safe: When done correctly, SODIS effectively reduces the presence of pathogens, including bacteria, viruses, and protozoa, improving the overall safety of drinking water.

Limitations of SODIS

Weather Dependent: The effectiveness of SODIS is contingent on sunny conditions. Overcast or rainy days prolong the treatment time or may render it ineffective. To overcome this, water can be treated over two consecutive days if sunlight is not intense or consistent.

Water Clarity: SODIS is less effective with turbid or colored water. Pre-filtering to remove sediments and debris is necessary to ensure clarity and effectiveness.

Limited Volume: The process typically treats water in small quantities (the size of the bottle). Implementing a rotation system or using multiple bottles can help increase the daily treated water volume.

Bottle Degradation: Plastic bottles can degrade over time, especially with prolonged exposure to sunlight. Regularly inspecting and replacing bottles as needed ensures the process remains effective.

Creative Uses

In gardening, using SODIS-treated water for irrigation can benefit plant health. This is especially useful in regions where water quality is compromised. Clean, purified water ensures that plants are not exposed to harmful pathogens or contaminants, promoting healthier growth and reducing the risk of soil contamination.

In emergency situations or remote outdoor adventures, SODIS becomes an invaluable resource. It offers an effective way to purify drinking water when standard treatment methods are unavailable, such as during natural disasters or while camping in the wilderness.

Additionally, SODIS can serve as a source of clean water for washing vegetables or cleaning. Adopting SODIS in daily life can be a small but impactful step towards a more sustainable lifestyle.

7

NO-GRID COOKING WITH STORED HEAT

USE A DIY THERMAL COOKER TO RETAIN
HEAT AND FINISH COOKING MEALS WITHOUT
CONTINUOUS ENERGY

Imagine a cooking method that's eco-friendly, energy-efficient, and still whips up delicious meals — that's the magic of a DIY thermal cooker. It's not just about cooking; it's about embracing a creative way of preparing your food.

By harnessing the power of retained heat, a thermal cooker allows you to bring your meal to a boil using conventional methods, then continue the cooking process without any extra energy. Think of it as a slow cooker without the plug. This method is a game-changer for those who love the depth of flavor that slow cooking brings but are also conscious about energy use. Whether you're simmering a stew or cooking rice, once you've transferred your dish into a thermal cooker, it continues to cook gently, melding flavors and tenderizing ingredients to perfection.

How Does It Work?

At the heart of thermal cooking is the science of heat retention. Here's the deal: every cooking method involves transferring heat to food. Usually, this heat dissipates over time, requiring a continuous energy source. But what if you could capture this initial heat and make it last longer? Enter insulation — the superhero of thermal cooking. Good insulation acts like a snug blanket around your pot, slowing down the loss of heat and keeping your food cooking longer without additional energy. The better the insulation, the more effective the cooker.

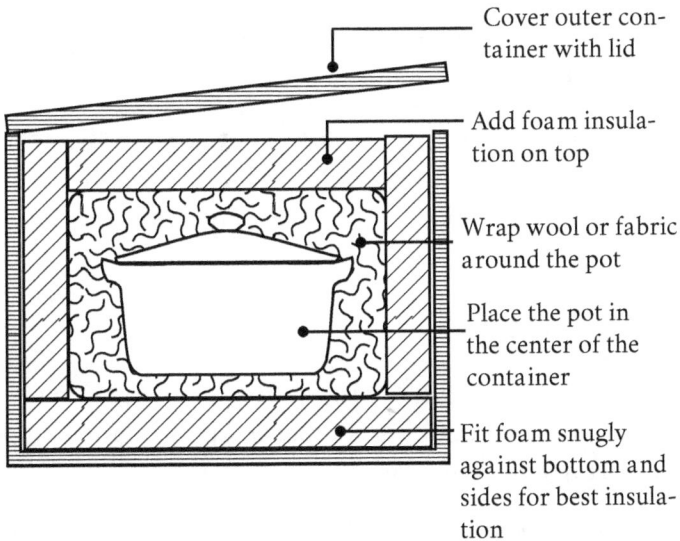

Cover outer container with lid

Add foam insulation on top

Wrap wool or fabric around the pot

Place the pot in the center of the container

Fit foam snugly against bottom and sides for best insulation

Materials Needed

Here's what to gather to ensure your cooker is not just effective but also a joy to use:

Insulation Materials

Polystyrene Sheets or Foam: These materials are great for trapping heat due to their low thermal conductivity.

Wool or Thick Fabric: If you're looking for something more natural, wool or layers of thick fabric can also serve as good second layer insulators.

Containers

Large Pot with Lid: This will be where you initially heat your food. It should be large enough to accommodate your meals and have a tight-fitting lid to retain steam and heat.

Insulated Outer Container: This could be a cooler, large enough to accommodate the pot with extra room for insulation. Alternatively, a sturdy box or basket can be adapted to serve as the outer container.

Lid or Cover for the Outer Container: To seal the heat in, you'll need a lid or cover. This could be the existing lid of a cooler or a custom-made cover that fits snugly over your chosen outer container.

Heat Source

Stove or Heat Plate: Before the food goes into the thermal cooker, it needs to reach cooking temperature. A regular kitchen stove or a portable heat plate will do the trick.

Selecting the Right Materials

Efficiency is Key: The efficiency of your thermal cooker relies heavily on the quality of insulation. Look for materials that have good insulation properties and are also durable.

Safety Considerations: Ensure that all materials are safe to use and won't melt, off-gas, or become flammable when in contact with heat.

Accessibility: Consider using materials that are readily available or that you already have at home. Recycling old wool blankets or repurposing a cooler can be both cost-effective and environmentally friendly.

Building Your Cooker

Now that you've got all your materials, it's time to build your very own thermal cooker. Follow these steps to ensure an effective, portable, and durable cooker:

1. Assemble Your Outer Container:

Choose an outer container that is larger than your inner pot, leaving enough room for insulation.

Line the bottom of the outer container with a layer of polystyrene, or foam (at least 1.5 inches thick). This layer acts as the base insulation.

2. Insulate the Sides:

Cut your insulation material to fit the sides of the outer container. If you're using polystyrene or foam, measure and cut precise panels.

Fit the insulation snugly against the sides, ensuring there are no gaps where heat could escape.

3. Add a Second Layer of Insulation:

For better insulation, layer fabric or wool around the sides as a second layer.

4. Place the Inner Pot:

Heat your food in the inner pot on your regular stove or heat plate until it reaches the desired temperature and begins cooking.

Carefully place the hot inner pot into the center of the insulated outer container.

5. Seal the Top:

Add a layer of fabric or wool on top of the pot, then add the foam insulation on top.

Close the outer container with its lid or cover. If it doesn't have a tight seal, consider adding more insulating fabric over the top before closing.

6. Making It Portable and Durable:

Handles: Add handles or straps to the outer container if it doesn't have them, ensuring they're securely attached and capable of carrying the weight.

Weatherproofing: If you plan to use your thermal cooker outdoors, consider weatherproofing the outer container with a water-resistant coating or cover.

Recipes and Cooking Techniques

Specially Adapted Recipes for a Thermal Cooker

Cooking with a thermal cooker requires recipes that can withstand and benefit from slow, gradual cooking. Here are some ideas:

Grains and Legumes: Hearty and absorbent, grains and legumes like rice, quinoa, lentils, and beans are ideal for thermal cooking.

They absorb flavors well and become tender over the extended cooking period.

Soups: Recipes like vegetable stew or soup are perfect, as the slow cooking allows for deep flavor development.

Porridge and Oats: Start your day with a warm, hearty bowl of porridge or oats, prepared in your thermal cooker.

Here are some recipes for your DIY thermal cooker:

Hearty Vegetable Lentil Soup

Ingredients:
- 1 cup lentils (rinsed)
- 4 cups vegetable broth
- 1 onion, diced
- 2 carrots, diced
- 2 stalks celery, diced
- 2 cloves garlic, minced
- 1 can diced tomatoes
- 1 teaspoon thyme
- Salt and pepper to taste

Instructions:

1. In a large pot, sauté onions, carrots, and celery until slightly softened. Add garlic and cook for another minute.

2. Add the lentils, vegetable broth, diced tomatoes, and thyme. Bring to a boil.

3. Once boiling, carefully transfer the pot into your preheated DIY thermal cooker.

4. Seal the cooker and let it sit for 4-6 hours, allowing the lentils to become tender and the flavors to meld.

5. Before serving, check the seasoning and adjust with salt and pepper.

Chickpea Tomato Pasta

Ingredients:
- 2 cups of your favorite pasta
- 1 can chickpeas, drained and rinsed
- 1 can diced tomatoes
- 2 cloves garlic, minced
- 1 onion, diced
- 2 tablespoons olive oil
- Salt and pepper to taste
- Fresh basil for garnish

Instructions:

1. In a pot, heat olive oil at medium heat. Add onions and garlic, cooking until they're soft and fragrant.

2. Add the canned tomatoes, chickpeas, and pasta. Pour in enough water to cover all the ingredients, usually about 2 cups. Season with salt and pepper.

3. Bring the mixture to a boil, ensuring the pasta is fully submerged.

4. Once boiling, transfer the pot to your preheated DIY thermal cooker.

5. Seal the cooker and let it sit for about 2-3 hours. The pasta will cook and absorb the tomato flavors.

6. Serve garnished with fresh basil.

Basic Quinoa Pilaf

Ingredients:

- 1 cup quinoa, rinsed and drained
- 2 cups vegetable broth or water
- 1 onion, finely chopped
- 1 bell pepper, diced
- 1 carrot, diced
- 1 teaspoon olive oil
- 1/2 teaspoon garlic powder
- Salt and pepper to taste

Instructions:

1. Heat olive oil over medium heat in a pot. Add onions, bell pepper, and carrots, sautéing until they are soft.

2. Stir in the quinoa, vegetable broth, garlic powder, salt, and pepper.

3. Bring the mixture to a boil, then carefully transfer the pot to your preheated DIY thermal cooker.

4. Seal the cooker and let it sit for 3-4 hours until the quinoa is fluffy and all the liquid is absorbed.

5. Fluff with a fork and serve as a simple yet nutritious side dish or foundation for other toppings.

Coconut Rice Pudding

Ingredients:

- 1 cup rice (short-grain or Arborio rice works well)
- 4 cups coconut milk (or a mix of coconut milk and water)
- 1/3 cup sugar
- 1/2 teaspoon vanilla extract
- A pinch of salt
- Optional: raisins or cinnamon for added flavor

Instructions:

1. In your pot, combine the rice, coconut milk, sugar, vanilla extract, and a pinch of salt.

2. Bring the mixture to a boil while stirring occasionally to ensure the sugar dissolves and the rice doesn't stick.

3. Once boiling, transfer the pot to your preheated DIY thermal cooker.

4. Seal the cooker and let it sit for 5-6 hours. The rice will slowly absorb the coconut milk, becoming creamy and tender.

5. Serve warm or cold, garnished with raisins or a sprinkle of cinnamon if desired.

Remember, the key to successful thermal cooking is bringing the food to the right initial temperature and then allowing ample time for the ingredients to cook through slowly in the retained heat. Enjoy experimenting with these recipes and savor the delicious, energy-efficient meals they produce.

Maximizing Efficiency

To truly harness the power of your DIY thermal cooker, consider these strategies for peak efficiency:

Check for Gaps: Make sure there are no gaps or holes where heat could escape. The more sealed the environment, the better it will retain heat.

Maximize Insulation: Don't skimp on insulation materials. The thicker and more insulating the material, the better it will retain heat.

Pre-Heat Your Pot: Consider warming your inner pot before

adding your food to give an extra boost of retained heat.

Optimal Fill Levels: Fill your inner pot to an optimal level, usually about two-thirds full. This ensures enough heat is retained around the food for even cooking.

Pre-Heat Your Container: Warm up the insulated container before adding your hot pot. This can be done by placing a container of hot water inside it for a few minutes, then removing it just before you add your cooking pot.

Adjust Cooking Times: Understand that cooking times will vary depending on the initial temperature of the food, the amount of food, and the effectiveness of your insulation. It might take a few tries to get the timing right for different dishes.

Modify Recipes: Adapt recipes for longer cooking times and less liquid evaporation. If a recipe typically requires simmering to reduce liquid, reduce the liquid amount when using a thermal cooker as there will be minimal evaporation.

Maintenance and Safety

Cleaning: Regularly clean the inner cooking pot as you would with any cookware. The insulated container should be kept dry and clean — a quick wipe after use usually suffices.

Inspection: Periodically check the insulation for any signs of wear or damage, replacing materials as needed.

Food Safety: Always ensure food reaches a safe temperature before placing it into the thermal cooker to avoid bacterial growth.

Handling Hot Items: Use caution when handling the hot inner pot, and always secure the lid tightly to avoid spills or leaks.

8

NATURAL SOLUTIONS FOR HOUSEHOLD PESTS

USE NATURAL REMEDIES FOR PEST CONTROL LIKE
NEEM OIL OR DIATOMACEOUS EARTH

Homemade pest control methods aren't just about keeping unwanted critters at bay; they're about doing so in a way that's safe for your plants and your family. Imagine using ingredients that are often already in your cupboard or can be easily found at your local store. For safe pest control, you can commonly use neem oil and diatomaceous earth.

Neem oil is a powerhouse in the garden, known for its ability to deter a wide range of pests. Then there's diatomaceous earth, a powdery substance that works wonders by physically deterring insects.

Why Choose Natural Pest Control?

Natural pest control works harmoniously with the environment, breaking down quickly and posing minimal risk to non-target species. By choosing ingredients like neem oil, you're using a product that's been used safely for centuries, known for its efficacy and minimal environmental footprint. Diatomaceous earth offers a physical barrier against pests, not a toxic one, ensuring that your garden remains a safe place for all.

Common Ingredients and Their Uses

Navigating the world of homemade pest control means getting familiar with some of the most effective, natural allies in your fight against unwanted garden invaders. Let's explore how they work and what they target:

Neem Oil

Extracted from the neem tree, neem oil is a versatile and potent organic pesticide and insect repellent. It works in several ways: by inhibiting the feeding and growth of pests, disrupting their life cycle, and repelling them with its strong scent. It's particularly effective against aphids, mites, scale, and whiteflies, among others. To use, mix with water and a little mild soap (which helps it stick to the leaves) and spray onto affected plants. Be sure to apply during cooler parts of the day to avoid leaf burn.

Diatomaceous Earth

This powder is made from the fossilized remains of small aquatic organisms known as diatoms. The microscopic edges are sharp and abrasive, making it lethal to insects. When they crawl over it, it damages their exoskeletons and makes them to dehydrate and die. It's particularly effective against slugs, beetles, and other crawling pests. Sprinkle a thin layer around the base of plants or on the leaves. While it's non-toxic to humans and animals, it's best to use food-grade diatomaceous earth and avoid inhaling the dust.

Other Natural Ingredients

Vinegar: With its acetic acid content, vinegar can act as a herbicide. When applied directly, it can help manage weeds but be cautious, as it can harm your plants too.

Essential Oils: Many pests are deterred by the strong scents of certain essential oils. Peppermint, eucalyptus, and citronella can repel ants, spiders, and even rodents. Mix a few drops with water and spray around affected areas.

Soap Solution: A simple mix of natural soap and water can be an effective insecticide against a variety of pests. The soap suffocates the pests by breaking down their protective waxy coating. Use a mild, natural soap to avoid harming plants.

Remember, the key to pest control is regular monitoring and early intervention. Keep an eye on your plants, and at the first sign of trouble, reach for these natural solutions.

Creating Your Homemade Pest Solutions

Here are some recipes and tips to prepare effective remedies for a variety of pests:

Neem Oil Spray

For a broad range of insects including aphids, mites, and scale:

Mix 2 teaspoons of neem oil with 1 teaspoon of mild liquid soap.

Add this mixture to 1 quart of water and stir well.

Pour the mixture into a spray bottle and apply generously to affected areas of plants, covering all surfaces.

Apply every 1-2 weeks or after heavy rain.

Diatomaceous Earth Application

For slugs, beetles, and other crawling pests:

Ensure you are using food-grade diatomaceous earth.

Lightly sprinkle a thin layer around the base of plants or directly onto the soil where pests are seen.

For leaf-eating insects, dust a fine layer on the foliage.

Reapply after rain or watering as it needs to be dry to be effective.

Vinegar Solution

For weeds and small fungal issues:

Mix 1 part water with 1 part vinegar.

For tough weeds, use vinegar undiluted.

Apply directly onto the weeds or areas affected by mold and fungi. Be cautious to avoid desired plants as it can harm them.

Use on a sunny day for the best effect as the sun activates the vinegar.

Essential Oil Repellent

For repelling a variety of insects and small rodents:

Choose essential oils like peppermint, citronella, or eucalyptus.

Mix 10-15 drops of essential oil with 1 quart of water.

Add a squirt of liquid soap to help the mixture adhere to surfaces.

Spray around the affected areas or potential entry points for pests.

Reapply weekly and after rain.

Soap Spray

For a variety of soft-bodied insects like aphids, mealybugs, and spider mites:

Mix 1.5 teaspoons of mild liquid soap with 1 quart of water.

Stir gently and pour into a spray bottle.

Coat the affected plants thoroughly, particularly the undersides of leaves where pests hide.

Repeat application every few days until the pests are gone.

Tips for Effective Application and Frequency

Always test a small part of the plant first before applying any solution to the entire plant. Wait 24-48 hours to check for adverse reactions.

Apply sprays in the early morning or late afternoon to avoid the hot sun which can cause plants to burn, especially when wet.

Be consistent and patient. Natural remedies often require regular application and time to see results.

Keep a close eye on the plants for signs of pests and act promptly. Early intervention is key to preventing infestations.

Whether dealing with a sudden aphid attack or an ongoing battle against slugs, these recipes will arm you with the tools you need to keep your garden healthy and thriving.

Integrated Pest Management Strategies

Integrated Pest Management (IPM) is a holistic approach that combines various strategies to manage pests effectively and sustainably. It's not just about reacting to pests; it's about creating an environment less conducive to their proliferation. Here's how you can integrate IPM strategies with your homemade solutions:

Combining Homemade Solutions with Physical Barriers

Netting and Row Covers: Protect your plants with physical barriers. Fine netting or row covers can prevent pests from reaching your plants while still allowing light and water through.

Traps: Use traps for specific pests. Sticky traps can catch flying insects, while bait traps can be effective for slugs and snails.

Garden Practices

Crop Rotation: Change where you plant certain types of crops each year to disrupt the life cycles of pests that prefer specific plants.

Companion Planting: Some plants can repel pests naturally and can be planted alongside more vulnerable crops as a protective measure.

Regular Cleaning: Remove plant debris and diseased plants promptly. Cleanliness can greatly reduce pest populations by removing their habitats and food sources.

Understanding Pest Life Cycles

Learn about the pests that are common in your area and understand their life cycles. Knowing when pests are most vulnerable or most active can help you time your interventions for maximum effect.

Monitor the garden regularly for signs of pests. Early detection is key to preventing small problems from becoming big infestations.

Implementing Preventative Measures

Maintain healthy soil with good fertility and moisture management. Healthy plants are less vulnerable to pests.

Encourage natural predators in your garden, such as ladybugs, lacewings, and birds, by providing habitats and avoiding broad-spectrum pesticides.

By incorporating these IPM strategies, you're not just tackling pests; you're cultivating a resilient garden ecosystem. With IPM, pest management becomes less about constant battle and more about smart, sustainable stewardship.

Safety and Precautions

While natural remedies for pest control are generally safer than chemical alternatives, it's important to handle and apply them with care. Always wear gloves when working with substances like neem oil or diatomaceous earth, and avoid inhaling any powders. When creating and applying sprays, do so in a ventilated area and avoid direct contact with your skin and eyes. It's also crucial to keep all homemade pest solutions clearly labeled and stored out of reach from children and pets.

When using these remedies in your garden or home, consider the presence of pets and children. Ensure that the application sites are inaccessible or apply the remedies during times when exposure risk is minimal. Educate family members about what you're using and why, emphasizing the importance of not touching or ingesting any substances used for pest control.

Troubleshooting and Adjusting Your Approach

Even with the best preparations, you might encounter issues with your natural pest control methods. If you're not seeing the desired results, first reconsider the application frequency and ensure you're applying the remedy at optimal times, such as early morning or late evening. Check if the concentration of your solution is appropriate; sometimes, a stronger or weaker solution might be more effective. Also, remember that environmental factors like rain can wash away your applications. Don't hesitate to switch methods or combine different strategies if one isn't working. Pest control often requires a flexible, observant approach, ready to adapt to changing conditions and pest behaviors.

9

QUART-SIZE HERB GARDENS ON COUNTERTOPS

USE MASON JARS TO CREATE A COMPACT INDOOR
HERB GARDEN

Imagine having a little green oasis right on your windowsill or kitchen counter, filled with herbs just waiting to be plucked and added to your favorite dishes. Mason jar herb gardens offers a compact solution for growing herbs indoors.

Whether you're in an apartment with limited space or just love the idea of a mini-garden, Mason jars provide the perfect vessel for your culinary greenery. They're easy to set up, versatile, and add a touch of green to any space. Plus, there's something satisfying about using herbs that you've grown yourself.

Selecting Your Herbs

Choosing the right herbs is crucial for a thriving mini garden. The good news is, many herbs are well-suited for growing in confined spaces and will flourish in your jars.

Herbs Suitable for Mason Jar Growing

Basil: Basil is a favorite for Mason jar gardens. It needs plenty of sunlight and regular harvesting to keep it bushy.

Mint: Vigorous and easy to grow, mint is perfect for beginners.

Cilantro: If you love fresh salsa, cilantro can be a great addition to your jar garden. It enjoys cooler temperatures and ample light.

Parsley: Both curly and flat-leaf varieties do well in jars.

Chives: With their onion flavor, chives are both decorative and delicious. They're hardy and grow well in moderate light.

Tips for Choosing Herbs

Consider Sunlight: Before picking your herbs, consider the amount of sunlight your space receives. Herbs like basil and cilantro will need a sunny spot, while others may tolerate lower light conditions.

Think About Flavor: Choose herbs you love to cook with. If you're a fan of Italian food, basil and parsley might be your go-tos. Love making tea? Mint could be perfect.

Understand Your Space: Be realistic about how many jars and plants your space can accommodate. It's better to have a few healthy plants than too many crowded together.

Gathering Supplies

Here's what you'll need to start your indoor garden:

Mason Jars: You can use any size, but quart-sized jars are usually the most versatile. Wide-mouth jars are easier to work with when planting and harvesting your herbs.

Soil: A quality potting mix is essential for healthy herbs. Look for a mix that's well-draining and nutrient-rich, suitable for container gardening.

Seeds or Starter Plants: Decide whether you want to start from seeds or use starter plants from your local nursery. Seeds might take longer to grow, but watching them sprout is part of the fun!

Gravel or Pebbles: These are crucial for drainage at the bottom of your jars. They help keep water from sitting at the roots, which can cause rot.

When selecting your Mason jars, consider the mature size of the herbs you want to grow. Larger herbs like basil might be happier in a bigger jar, while smaller herbs like thyme can thrive in something smaller. Transparent jars make it easy to keep an eye on the moisture levels in the soil, but if you're concerned about algae growth or just prefer a different look, you can paint or decorate the outside of your jars. Just remember, whatever size or type of jar you choose, cleanliness is crucial so be sure to start with jars that are thoroughly washed and dried.

Preparation

Now that you've gathered your supplies, it's time to prepare your Mason jars for planting:

1. Clean Your Jars: Start with clean, dry jars. Wash them in soapy water and rinse thoroughly. This step helps prevent any mold or bacteria from affecting your herbs.

2. Create Drainage: Add a 1-2 inch layer of gravel or pebbles to the bottom of each jar. This layer will help water drain away

from the roots, preventing root rot.

3. Add Soil: Fill the jars with potting mix, leaving an inch of space below the rim. This space allows room for watering and prevents soil from spilling out.

4. Plant Your Herbs

Seeds: If you're starting from seeds, sprinkle a few on the surface of the soil and cover them with a thin layer of soil. Water gently to moisten the soil without disturbing the seeds. Keep the soil moist until the seeds germinate.

Starter Plants: Gently remove the plant from its container and loosen the roots. Make a hole in the soil of your Mason jar large enough to accommodate the root ball. Place the plant in the hole and gently press the soil around it. Water immediately after planting to settle the soil around the roots.

Drainage is key in a Mason jar garden because unlike traditional pots, Mason jars don't have drainage holes. The layer of gravel or pebbles at the bottom is crucial to keep water from pooling around the roots. Additionally, be mindful of watering; it's better to water little and often, ensuring the soil is moist but not waterlogged. Over-watering is a common issue in container gardening, especially in non-draining containers, so keep a close eye on soil moisture.

Caring for Your Herbs

Caring for your Mason jar herbs is a joyful journey filled with little moments of wonder as you watch your greenery grow. Here's how you can ensure your mini garden flourishes:

Watering

Mason jar herb gardens don't have drainage holes, so it's crucial to water sparingly to prevent waterlogging. Check the soil moisture by sticking your finger about an inch deep. Water only when the top inch of soil feels dry.

When you do water, do so slowly and steadily until you can see moisture through the glass at the bottom layer of pebbles, indicating the entire soil column has been watered.

Consider using a spray bottle for gentle watering, especially for young, delicate plants.

Sunlight

Most herbs thrive in bright, indirect light. A sunny windowsill that gets a minimum of 6 hours of sunlight daily is ideal.

Rotate your jars every regularly to ensure all sides of the plant receive equal light, promoting even growth.

If natural light is limited, consider using a grow light to keep your herbs happy.

Common Care Tips

Keep an eye out for signs of stress, such as yellowing leaves or stunted growth. This could be due to overwatering, too little light, or nutrient deficiencies.

Every few weeks, feed your herbs with a diluted liquid fertilizer to replenish nutrients in the soil.

If algae start to form on the jar's interior due to light exposure, you can cover the jar with fabric or paint the outside to block light while still allowing you to remove the cover and check the soil moisture.

Pruning and Harvesting

Regular pruning encourages bushier, fuller growth. Snip off the top leaves and stems with a pair of clean scissors or just pinch them off with your fingers.

Always leave several sets of leaves on the plant so it can continue to photosynthesize and grow.

Harvest your herbs regularly but moderately. Taking too much at once can stress the plant and slow its growth.

For continuous yield, consider planting new seeds every few weeks so that as one jar begins to wane, another is reaching its peak.

Troubleshooting Common Problems

Even with the best care, you may encounter a few hiccups in your Mason jar herb garden. Here are some common issues and how to address them:

Inadequate Growth

Lighting: Ensure your herbs are getting enough light. If they're leggy or pale, they might need more sunlight. Move them to a sunnier spot or using a grow light.

Nutrients: If growth is slow and the leaves are yellowing, your herbs might be hungry. Feed them with a diluted liquid fertilizer every few weeks.

Root Space: As plants grow, they might become root-bound. If growth slows dramatically, consider transplanting them to a larger jar or pruning the roots slightly and replanting.

Pests and Diseases

Pests: Keep an eye out for pests like aphids or spider mites. If you spot any, try a gentle spray of soapy water or neem oil on the affected areas.

Diseases: Overwatering can lead to fungal diseases. Ensure the soil is well-draining and you're not watering too much. Remove any diseased leaves promptly to prevent spread.

Creative Ideas

Your Mason jar herb garden is a functional piece of living art, and there are plenty of ways to add personal touches:

Labels: Use stylish labels or tags to mark each herb. You can write on the jar with a chalk marker, use hanging tags, or even paint the names directly onto the jars.

Decorative Stones: Add a layer of decorative stones or colored pebbles for a pop of color and to help retain moisture.

Painted Jars: Give your jars a makeover with some non-toxic paint. Whether it's a full coat, some patterns, or just painting the bottom half, it'll add a unique touch while also helping to block out light and prevent algae growth.

Arrangement: Play with the arrangement of your jars. Grouping them together can create a lush, garden-like feel. Consider using a tiered shelf or hanging them at different levels with macrame hangers for a vertical garden effect.

10

SUN-FAST FOOD PRESERVATION

MAKE A SOLAR DEHYDRATOR TO PRESERVE FRUITS
AND VEGETABLES

Historically, our ancestors relied on the sun to dry foods for preservation, and today, we're rediscovering this method as a perfect antidote to the modern throwaway culture. Solar dehydrators are making a comeback, not just as a nod to tradition but as a practical, energy-efficient solution. They don't just preserve food; they lock in flavors and nutrients, all while using zero electricity.

How Does It Work?

At its core, dehydration is a simple yet effective method to preserve food. By removing moisture, it stops the growth of bacteria, yeasts, and molds that spoil food. Most microorganisms need water to thrive, and by decreasing the water content in food, you're essentially creating an environment where they can't survive. The result? Shelf-stable food that retains much of its original nutrients and flavor.

A solar dehydrator uses the sun's energy to raise the temperature inside a drying chamber. As the air heats up, it circulates around the food, drawing moisture out and carrying it away. But it's not just about heat; proper airflow is crucial to remove the moist air and bring in dry air to continue the process efficiently.

It's a clean, cost-effective way to dry food, reducing reliance on electric dehydrators. Plus, it's a gentle process, often resulting in higher quality dried foods with better retention of color, taste, and nutrients.

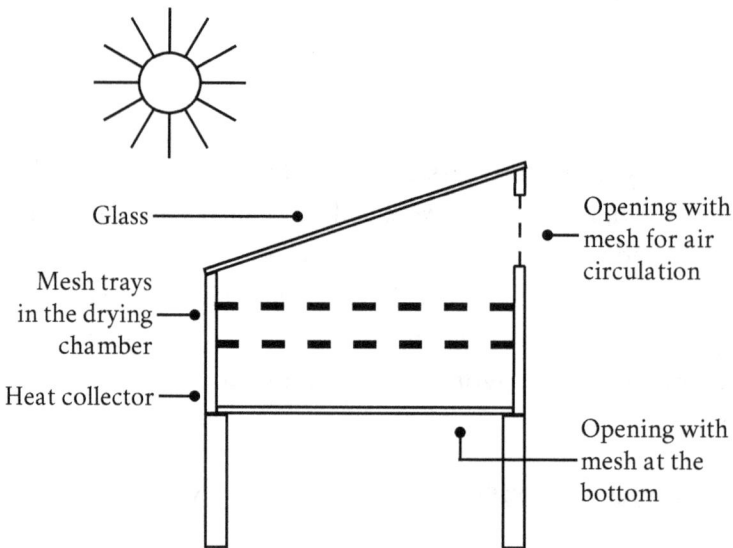

Designing Your Dehydrator

There are various models to consider, each with its own benefits. The most common types include the box dehydrator, which resembles a large wooden box with a clear top to let in sunlight, and the more compact, portable panel dehydrators. Some enthusiasts even create hybrid designs, combining elements from different models to suit their needs.

Factors to Consider in Design

Size: Consider how much food you plan to dehydrate at one time. A larger family might need a bigger dehydrator, while a smaller one might suffice for occasional use or limited space.

Materials: Most solar dehydrators are made from wood or plywood, with metal trays for holding the food. The cover should be a transparent, heat-resistant material like glass or clear polycarbonate to let in sunlight.

Location: The best spot for your dehydrator is one that receives maximum sunlight for the longest period during the day. South-facing locations typically work best in the Northern Hemisphere.

Basic Components

Heat Collector: This is the part of the dehydrator that captures and converts sunlight into heat. It's typically a flat, dark-colored surface that absorbs solar energy efficiently. Beneath the collector, there should be space for air to circulate and become heated before moving into the drying chamber.

Drying Chamber: This is where the food is placed on mesh trays. The chamber should be designed to maximize airflow around the food, ensuring even drying. The interior should be dark and made of non-toxic, heat-absorbing materials.

Vents: Proper ventilation is crucial. Vents or openings are typically placed at the lower end of the heat collector and at the top of the drying chamber. This setup creates a natural convection current, drawing in cooler air from the bottom, heating it, and then letting it rise through the chamber, carrying moisture away.

Mesh trays: These hold the food. They are often made from stainless steel or food-grade plastic. The design should allow for maximum exposure of food to the warm, dry air.

When designing your solar dehydrator, consider your personal needs, the climate you live in, and the resources available to you. With planning and a bit of DIY spirit, you'll be well on your way to enjoying sun-dried treats from your very own solar dehydrator.

Building Your Dehydrator

Building your own solar dehydrator is a rewarding DIY project that can provide you with a sustainable way to preserve food. Remember, this guide is just a starting point as specific size and measurement recommendations are not provided; we encourage you to let your creativity shine by designing a dehydrator that uniquely suits your space and needs.

Here's a basic guide to constructing a simple dehydrator:

Materials Needed:

- Wood or plywood for the frame

- Polycarbonate or glass for the cover

- Dark-colored metal sheet or black paint for the heat collector

- Stainless steel or food-grade plastic mesh for the trays

- Screws and nails for assembly

- Non-toxic paint or varnish for finishing

- Mesh for covering vents or openings

- Tools for cutting and assembling (saw, screwdriver, etc.)

Step-by-Step Instructions:

1. Design Your Dehydrator: Choose a design that suits your needs — a box or panel model is a good start. Sketch out your design, noting dimensions and materials needed.

2. Gather Materials: Collect all necessary materials, including wood for the frame, polycarbonate or glass for the cover, metal for the trays, screws, nails, and non-toxic paint or varnish.

3. Build the Frame: Cut the wood to the desired dimensions for the sides, bottom, and top of the dehydrator. Assemble the frame using screws or nails, ensuring it's sturdy and square.

4. Create the Heat Collector: Attach a dark-colored metal sheet or paint the bottom interior surface black to absorb heat. Ensure there are vents or openings below the collector for air to enter and heat up.

5. Add the Drying Chamber: Construct or adapt a compartment above the heat collector to hold the food trays. Ensure it's well sealed but allows for air circulation with vents or openings at the top.

6. Install Mesh Trays: Create or purchase trays that fit inside the drying chamber. They should be easy to slide in and out.

7. Cover with Transparent Material: Seal the top of the dehydrator with a transparent cover to allow sunlight in. Use screws to

secure the cover, ensuring it's tight and weather-resistant.

8. Cover Vents or Openings with Mesh: Install mesh over the vents or openings at the bottom of the heat collector and at the top of the drying chamber to prevent insects from entering.

9. Final Touches: Apply a non-toxic varnish or paint to protect the wood and improve the dehydrator's appearance.

Check all components are secure and the dehydrator is stable.

Tips for Effective Assembly and Maximizing Solar Exposure

Orientation: Position your dehydrator to face the sun's path — generally southward — to maximize exposure.

Angle: Consider the angle of the dehydrator's cover. Adjusting the angle according to your latitude can improve solar absorption.

Airflow: Ensure good airflow through the dehydrator for efficient drying. The air should enter cool at the bottom, heat up, and exit warm and moist at the top.

Safety Considerations

Material Safety: Use materials safe for food contact and exposure to high temperatures.

Stability: Ensure the dehydrator is stable and won't tip over in the wind.

Tool Safety: Use gloves, goggles, and other protective equipment when cutting wood or metal and assembling the dehydrator.

With these steps and considerations, you'll create a functional tool that dries food using the clean, renewable energy of the sun.

Preparing Food for Dehydration

Dehydrating food is a great way to preserve the bounty of your garden or local market. However, the preparation is key to ensuring the best results. Here's how to get your fruits and vegetables ready for dehydration:

Selecting the Right Fruits and Vegetables

Freshness Matters: Choose ripe, high-quality produce. Fresh fruits and vegetables are ideal candidates, such as apples, berries, grapes, tomatoes, and peppers.

Consider Varieties: Some varieties dehydrate better than others. For instance, Roma tomatoes have less moisture and are excellent for drying, while certain apple varieties retain their flavor well when dehydrated.

Pre-Treatment

Blanching: Vegetables like carrots, peas, and broccoli benefit from a quick blanching in boiling water followed by an ice bath. This process helps to preserve color, flavor, and nutrients when dehydrating.

Dipping: Fruits prone to browning like apples, pears, and peaches can be dipped in a mixture of lemon juice and water (or pure ascorbic acid) to prevent oxidation.

Syrup Blanching: For a sweeter treat and to preserve color, some fruits can be blanched in a light syrup solution.

Slicing and Layout

Thickness: Cut fruits and vegetables into even, thin slices or strips. Around 1/4 inch thickness is typically ideal for balancing drying time and texture.

Consistency: Keep the size and thickness consistent for even drying. Use a mandoline slicer or a sharp knife for uniform slices.

Layout: Arrange the slices in a single layer on the dehydrator trays, ensuring none of the pieces are overlapping or touching. This allows air to circulate freely around each piece, promoting even drying.

Preparing your produce correctly can greatly impact the quality of your dried foods. Properly selected, pre-treated, and sliced foods will dry more efficiently and retain better color, texture, and flavor.

Using and Maintaining Your Dehydrator

Here are some best practices to ensure you get the most out of your sun-powered dehydrator:

Loading and Monitoring

Arrange your prepared slices evenly across the trays, ensuring no overlap. The more space each piece has, the better the air can circulate and the faster they will dry.

Monitor the progress throughout the day, especially the first few times you use the dehydrator. Check the temperature and humidity levels if possible, as these will give you an indication of how quickly the food is drying.

Rotate the mesh trays occasionally to ensure even drying, especially if your dehydrator has hot spots or areas with less airflow.

Determining Dryness

The dryness of food can vary depending on your preference and the intended use. Generally, fruits should be pliable but not sticky, while vegetables should be brittle or crisp.

To test, remove a piece from the dehydrator, let it cool for a few minutes, then feel and bend it. Remember, food will seem softer while it's warm, so always test after it has cooled.

Over-drying is better than under-drying, as residual moisture can lead to spoilage.

Cleaning and Storing

After each use, remove any food particles from the trays and interior. A brush or cloth usually does the trick.

If trays are very dirty, wash with warm, soapy water and dry thoroughly before storing.

Store the dehydrator in a clean, dry place to prevent mold and mildew. Cover it to protect it from dust and insects.

Troubleshooting Common Issues

Inconsistent Drying: If you find some pieces aren't drying as quickly as others, try rearranging the trays or the pieces on the trays for more even exposure. Consistency in slicing will also help.

Too Slow: If drying is too slow, consider increasing the angle or repositioning the dehydrator to catch more direct sunlight. Also, check that vents are clear and allowing for adequate airflow.

Mold or Spoilage: If you notice mold or spoilage, it might be a sign of inadequate drying. Ensure pieces are fully dehydrated before storage. If the problem persists, try increasing drying time or cutting pieces thinner to speed up the process.

Remember, every climate and dehydrator is different. What works perfectly one day might need adjustment the next. Keep a log of your processes and outcomes to help refine your technique over time.

EMBRACING AN OFF-GRID LIFESTYLE

Throughout this book, we've explored a variety of sustainable tips, from water disinfection to creating a natural fridge. These methods show that living sustainably can be innovative, practical, and often quite simple.

What's great about adopting an off-grid lifestyle is the ripple effect small changes can have. Switching to DIY dehydrators or using natural cleaners might seem trivial, yet they contribute to significant energy savings and a reduction in waste. Each action is a step towards a more sustainable future.

This book is just the beginning of your sustainable living journey. There's a wealth of knowledge to explore and new practices to adopt. The realm of off-grid living is filled with opportunities for continued learning and innovation. Keep exploring and remain open to trying new sustainable practices.

Incorporating off-grid hacks into your life is about more than survival or frugality; It's about making conscious choices that align with your values and finding joy in the simplicity of your actions. Whether you're in a rural area, embracing the full off-grid lifestyle, or in an urban environment, integrating bits and pieces of sustainable living, every effort counts.

Thank you for reading this book. May it be the start, not the end, of your journey towards self-sufficiency.

SHARE YOUR THOUGHTS

As you come to the end of this book, we hope it has offered you information and strategies for your no-grid survival journey, and we would be honored to hear your thoughts.

Please consider leave an honest review of this book on the store where you bought it. Your feedback is not only crucial to us but also to other readers interested in a self-sufficient lifestyle. Whether it's an insight you found useful, a story you'd like to share, or suggestions for future editions, your voice matters.

Thank you for choosing this book, and for taking the time to help us improve. Your support is greatly appreciated!

www.ingramcontent.com/pod-product-compliance
Lightning Source LLC
Chambersburg PA
CBHW060255030426

42335CB00014B/1704